Atlanta

Travel Guide

Quick Trips Series

Table of Contents

ATLANTA   6

🌐 CUSTOMS & CULTURE 7

🌐 GEOGRAPHY...10

🌐 WEATHER & BEST TIME TO VISIT 11

SIGHTS & ACTIVITIES: WHAT TO SEE & DO   13

🌐 GEORGIA AQUARIUM..13

🌐 STONE MOUNTAIN 14

🌐 HIGH MUSEUM OF ART...16

🌐 MARTIN LUTHER KING, JR. NATIONAL HISTORIC SITE & SWEET AUBURN DISTRICT 18

🌐 ATLANTA CYCLORAMA & CIVIL WAR MUSEUM 20

🌐 WORLD OF COCA COLA 22

🌐 BOTANICAL GARDEN...23

🌐 ATLANTA HISTORY CENTER 25

🌐 CHILDREN'S MUSEUM OF ATLANTA 27

🌐 ZOO ATLANTA..28

🌐 FERNBANK MUSEUM OF NATURAL HISTORY.......................29

🌐 CARTER CENTER & PRESIDENTIAL LIBRARY.......................31

🌐 CNN CENTER & STUDIO TOUR 33

🌐 CENTENNIAL OLYMPIC PARK..35

BUDGET TIPS 37

🌐 ACCOMMODATION 37

Super 8 Atlanta Airport Hotel.......................................37
Marriott Atlanta Airport 39
Crown Plaza Ravinia 40
Highland Inn 41
Days Inn, Atlanta Marietta Galleria...........................42

🌐 RESTAURANTS, CAFÉS & BARS.............................43

Sun Dial Restaurant, Bar & View...............................43
Alma Cocina 45
Anis Café & Bistro 46
Alfredo's Italian Restaurant.......................................47
Aja...47
Aqua Blue Restaurant & Bar 48

🌐 SHOPPING 49

Junkman's Daughter..49
Fab'rik 50
North Georgia Premium Outlets.................................51
Cumberland Mall 52
Lenox Square 53

KNOW BEFORE YOU GO 55

🌐 ENTRY REQUIREMENTS 55

🌐 HEALTH INSURANCE 56

🌐 TRAVELING WITH PETS 57

🌐 AIRPORTS..59

🌐 AIRLINES 63

🌐 HUBS 67

🌐 SEAPORTS 69

🌐 MONEY MATTERS 70

🌐 CURRENCY 70

🌐 Banking/ATMs 71

🌐 Credit Cards 72

🌐 Tourist Tax 72

🌐 Sales Tax 73

🌐 Tipping 75

🌐 Connectivity 76

🌐 Mobile Phones 76

🌐 Dialing Code 77

🌐 Emergency Numbers 78

🌐 General Information 78

🌐 Public Holidays 78

🌐 Time Zones 79

🌐 Daylight Savings Time 81

🌐 School Holidays 81

🌐 Trading Hours 82

🌐 Driving 82

🌐 Drinking 84

🌐 Smoking 85

🌐 Electricity 86

🌐 Food & Drink 87

🌐 American Sports 89

🌐 Useful Websites 92

Atlanta

Atlanta is the capital of Georgia and the state's largest

city. In the 1960s, during the civil rights movement,

Atlanta was dubbed "the city too busy to hate." Nowadays

it is known as "the city too busy to care" and Atlanta

stands tall as one of America's most modern and liveable

cities.

ATLANTA TRAVEL GUIDE

The Old Confederacy, the Civil Rights Movement, the Chattahoochee River, Coca-Cola and the 1996 Centennial Olympics bring to mind this famous southern city.

Atlanta is located in the northern part of Georgia, and has been the transportation hub of the southeast since the days of the Civil War, when all five original rail lines were rebuilt after the city was burned down in 1864. By the turn of the century there were fifteen rail lines.

Atlanta's Hartsfield-Atlanta International Airport is one of the busiest airports in the world. The city is the world headquarters of 13 Fortune 500 companies including Coca-Cola, CNN (Cable News Network), and UPS (United Parcel Service). MARTA is Atlanta's rapid-transit system, with four lines that run from north to south and east to west.

🌐 **Customs & Culture**

Before settlers started moving into the area in 1821, the land where Atlanta lies now belonged to the Creek and Cherokee Indians. There was a Creek village where Peachtree Creek flows into the Chattahoochee.

It was called, not surprisingly, Standing Peachtree. It was the closest Indian settlement to what we know now as metropolitan Atlanta. The settlers came in drones after the discovery of gold in the area. Then in 1843, the name of the town was changed to Marthasville as a way of honoring the governor's daughter – Martha – who had played a vital role in bringing the illustrious railroad to the area. Then in 1837 Atlanta was first founded and named as the end of Western & Atlantic railroad line. Ten years later, it was incorporated as a city.

Today, Atlanta has become the face of the new south. The city has a rich heritage with historical significance, yet is a fast-paced, modern metropolis.

Coca-Cola was established in Atlanta in 1892 when an entrepreneur named Asa Candler paid $2,300 to John S. Pemberton, a pharmacist who had first invented Coca-Cola to act as a headache and hangover tonic.

The Center for Disease Control (CDC) was established in Atlanta in 1946. You can drive on Auburn Avenue where Dr. Martin Luther King, Jr. was born and raised.

ATLANTA TRAVEL GUIDE

Underground Atlanta was opened in 1969 and played a key role in putting the city on the entertainment map.

Atlanta is the home of the Atlanta Symphony Orchestra which has received a number of international accolades, and the Atlanta Ballet which is the oldest professional dance company in America. It is also home to the Atlanta Braves baseball team, the Falcons football team, and the Hawks basketball team.

There are several festivals held in Atlanta. The Dogwood Festival and the Atlanta Jazz Festival are both held in the springtime. The Dogwood Festival is an annual arts and crafts festival and it is held in early April when the dogwoods are blooming. The summer brings the Atlanta Food & Wine Festival in May or June. The Virginia-

Highland Festival Summerfest is held in August. The Taste of Atlanta festival occurs in the fall, usually in October.

🌐 Geography

Atlanta lies in the northern part of Georgia and has a population of 432,000. It is the ninth largest metropolitan area in the US. The city is marked by hills and dense tree coverage and has been called "a city in a forest" because of the abundance of trees that cover the area. It covers about 132 square miles (342 km^2). It lies at the foot of the Appalachian Mountains. The major stream that runs through the city is the Peachtree Creek which flows for 7.5 miles (12.2km) due west.

ATLANTA TRAVEL GUIDE

Atlanta has over 300 parks, preserves, and gardens, and a non-profit organization called Trees Atlanta has made it its mission since 1985 to plant shade trees in Atlanta and has planted over 75,000 in the metropolitan area.

Jogging is a popular pastime and Atlanta hosts the Peachtree road race every year on Independence Day. Atlanta is also famous for its golf, for which it has 6 public golf courses, and tennis. There are facilities all along the Chattahoochee River which caters to an assortment of watersports, such as kayaking, canoeing, fishing, boating, and tubing. You can also take a balloon ride which offers incredible views of the Appalachians, the Atlanta skyline, Kennesaw Mountain north of Atlanta, St. Mountain which lies northeast of Atlanta, and Lake Lanier which is southeast of Hartsfield-Jackson International Airport.

🌏 Weather & Best Time to Visit

http://www.weather.com/weather/tenday/Atlanta+GA+US

GA0028

Lying at a high elevation of 1050ft (320m) above sea level makes the climate in Atlanta hot and humid in the summer and mild and temperamental in the winter. The average temperature in July may reach as high as 90F (32C) and in January it can dip to 43.5C (6.4F) with the suburbs reaching a little lower. Rainfall is abundant and is mainly concentrated in the seasons of winter and summer.

April, May, and October are considered to be the best weather months in Atlanta as the spring and fall seasons are long and gentle. The weather is good for outdoor and cultural activities year-round.

Sights & Activities: What to See & Do

🌑 Georgia Aquarium

225 Baker St NW

Atlanta, GA 30313

+1 404-581-4151

http://www.georgiaaquarium.org/

The Georgia Aquarium is the world's largest aquarium.

ATLANTA TRAVEL GUIDE

The aquarium holds beluga whales, whale sharks, and penguins.

It is also where you will enjoy various aquatic animals from all over the world. The aquarium holds many events like swimming with whale sharks, diving with whale sharks, birthday parties, and an exciting behind the scenes tours. There is an AT&T Dolphin Tales exhibit where you would find a coldwater quest, an ocean voyager, a tropical diver and a 4D Theater. This exhibit also has dancing dolphins, live actors and elaborate costumes that is guaranteed to entertain you.

Admission is $29.95 for adults, $23.95 for children (ages3-12), and $25.95 for seniors (age +65).

🌑 Stone Mountain

Stone Mountain Park

PO Box 778

Stone Mountain Park, GA 30086

+1-800-401-2407

http://www.stonemountainpark.com/

Stone Mountain is the world's largest piece of exposed

granite rock. It is also the longest running laser show with

some of the most awe-inspiring effects and graphics

mixed in with multi-dimensional magical enhancements.

The park has many family-oriented activities, lodging and

camping, and many other special events.

While visiting the park, you can go on the Great

Locomotive Adventure, take a ride on the Scenic

Railroad, or visit the town of Crossroads set in the 1870s where you will be able to view live shows, do some shopping and enjoy a fine dining experience.

There is also Geyser Towers which joins two thrilling adventures into one. You can enjoy the thrill of a water park merged with a multi-level ropes course.

The most basic way to enter the park is to purchase an adventure pass which costs $28 +tax for adults and $22 +tax for children ages 3-11. The pass includes admission to the Geyser Towers, SkyHike, Camp Highland Outpost, Journey 2: The Mysterious Island – The 4-D Experience, Scenic Railroad, Mini-Golf, Summit Skyride, Antebellum Plantation, Discovering Stone Mountain Museum at Memorial Hall, and The Great Barn. There is also live entertainment depending on the season, and if you add some extra dollars to your pass, you can add Ride the

Ducks on the date of your visit.

🌐 High Museum of Art

1280 Peachtree Street NE, Atlanta, GA 30309

+1-404-733-4444

www.high.org

The leading art museum in the southeastern United

States makes visitors and staff of the High Museum of Art

brim with excitement and jubilee. The museum – which

locals refer to as the High – has more than 13,000 works

of art in permanent collections. It also has an extensive

anthology of American art in the 19th and 20th centuries. It

also holds European paintings of significant stature,

decorative art, an African American art collection which is growing in size and stature, and so much more.

The High puts a strong emphasis on supporting works by Southern artists which is why it holds a growing collection of art work by Southern artists. It is the only major museum in the continent of North America that has a curatorial department that is specifically devoted to folk art and art that is self-taught.

The museum's regular operating hours are from 10am to 5pm on Tuesdays and Wednesdays, from 10am to 8pm on Thursdays, from 10am to 5pm on Fridays and Saturdays, and from 12 noon to 5pm on Sundays. The High is closed on Mondays and holidays. Admission is

$18 for adults, $15 for students and senior citizens.

Children can enter for free.

🌐 Martin Luther King, Jr. National Historic Site & Sweet Auburn District

450 Auburn Ave NE, Atlanta, GA 30312

+1 404-331-5190

http://www.nps.gov/malu/index.htm

Admission and parking are free. Tours fill up quickly as only 15 people are allowed on each tour so make sure to get there early in the day. If you're going in a group of 45 or less, you can reserve up to 3 spaces on the day of your tour.

ATLANTA TRAVEL GUIDE

This district was booming and blooming back in the 60s. It was also a thriving center for Atlanta's black enterprise from even before that dating back from the 1890s. Here, you can explore the birth home of Martin Luther King, Jr. You can visit the historic Ebenezer Baptist Church where King, Sr. served as pastor from 1931 until 1975. Dr. King, Jr. served as co-pastor with his father from 1960 until his assassination in 1968. Alberta King, Dr. King's mother, was the musical director at the church. You will also visit The King Center where you get a chance to see Dr. King's Nobel Peace Prize on display. The crypt and grave site of Dr. King and his wife, Coretta are also there.

There are two main two tours: the Birth Home Tour where you take a stroll around Dr. King's home from age twelve.

It's a thirty-minute tour and is available on a first-come, first-serve basis.

The second tour is the Encounter History Presentation which illustrates the historical significances the shaped the legacy of the great Dr. King. It is also a thirty-minute tour. There is also a DREAM gallery, a "Courage to Lead" exhibition, and an exhibition showing wax figurines of the freedom road marchers.

If you're visiting with young kids aged 9 to 12, they can ask to become Junior Rangers at the park which requires the kids to complete certain activities in an official activity booklet. When the kids finish the activities, they automatically become Junior Rangers. They also have to agree to live by the Junior Ranger Promise and Dr. King's Six Principles of Nonviolence

The historic park opens from 9am until 5pm every day during the winter operating season which starts from September 4th until May 27th. The summer operating hours are from 9am until 6pm daily and that's from May 28th until September 3rd.

🌏 Atlanta Cyclorama & Civil War Museum

800 Cherokee Ave SE, Atlanta, GA 30315

+1 404-658-7625

http://www.atlantacyclorama.org/

The Cyclorama is the largest diorama painting in the world. It stands at 42ft (12.8m) tall and is 358ft (109.12m) in circumference. It weighs 10,000lbs (4.5kg). This breath-taking painting offers viewers a breathtaking look into the Battle of Atlanta fought on July 22, 1864 during the Civil War in 1864. It is further enhanced by the addition of 3D figures in the foreground as well as terrain which uses authentic and unmistakable red clay of Georgia. The painting was first erected in 1893 at Grant Park.

There is also the Civil War Museum which houses artifacts from the time of the war and a steam locomotive named Texas, a veteran of the great locomotive chase of 1862.

The tour is actually a 2-part educational program on the Battle of Atlanta. You will spend 40 minutes learning new and interesting facts about the battle with thrilling enhancements like special lighting, sound effects, music and narration which is available in five languages;

English, French, German, Japanese, and Spanish.

Operating hours are from 9:30am until 4:30pm.

Admission for adults is $10.

🌐 World of Coca Cola

121 Baker St NW, Atlanta, GA 30313

+1 404-676-5151

http://www.worldofcoca-cola.com/

The fun-filled world of Coca Cola has numerous

attractions for the young and old. The attractions feature a

multi-sensory 4D theater, a soda fountain dating back

from the 1880s, a live action bottling line, and a chance to taste over 60 different drinks from all over the world.

There are also a variety of exhibits, tours and events. The World of Coca-Cola proudly supports teachers and the educational system. It provides teachers and schools with a reward system called 'My Coke Rewards' which help schools get the materials and provisions they need in order to facilitate the learning process and further enable young minds.

Admission for adults (13-64) is $16, for senior citizens (+65) is $14, and for youth (3-12) is $12. Toddlers up until two years old are free to enter with an adult. The hours of operation vary from day to day so be sure to call or check out their website when planning your visit.

🌐 Botanical Garden

1345 Piedmont Ave NE, Atlanta, GA 30309

+1 404-876-5859

http://www.atlantabotanicalgarden.org/

This enchanting garden full of blooming plants, greenery, and an adventure-filled and stimulating children's garden first opened its doors in 1973. The garden has more than 30 acres of gardens, forests, wildflower trails, a Canopy Walk that has a suspension bridge towering 40 ft (12.2m) into the air. The suspension bridge gives visitors the chance to walk through the treetops.

Each year with the turning of spring the Garden holds an annual celebration of flowers which takes place during the months of March and April called *Atlanta Blooms*. There is also a 10,000 square foot Fuqua Orchid Center and a Cascades Garden with a sanctuary and an outdoor kitchen called the Edible Garden. The types of gardens range from a Japanese Garden to a Rose Garden.

The Botanical Garden puts a strong emphasis on keeping kids safe and healthy, so if you have children in the mix, then cross the Flower Bridge and introduce them to the Children's Garden where the multitude of themed gardens and features will delight young and old.

This enchanted place has a Sunflower Fountain, a Laugh as well as a Live Garden, plus three other just as thrilling gardens, a tree house, and so much more. The Children's Garden lies on two acres and is built with the partnership of Children's Healthcare of Atlanta in an effort to emphasize wellness and healthy living.

Admission for adults is $18.95 and for children ages 3-12, admission is $12.95. Children under 3 years of age enter for free.

🌐 Atlanta History Center

130 West Paces Ferry Road NW, Atlanta, GA30305-1366

+1-404-814-4000

www.atlantahistorycenter.com

This center is much more than just a history center. It also holds 32 acres of gardens and wildlife trails as well as woodland areas. There is Southern folk art, exhibitions on the Civil War as well as on African-American heritage all displayed in the on-site museum and a wing specifically dedicated to the Centennial Olympic Games held in Atlanta in 1996. In addition, there is the Kenan Research Center and the Cherokee Garden Library.

There is also a souvenir shop and tours which will take you on a visit to the historic houses on location. These houses include the Tullie Smith Farm from the 1840s, the Swan House mansion which was fully restored in 1928, and the House and Museum of Margaret Mitchell, author of Gone with the Wind.

The museum's hours of operation are from 10am until 5:30pm from Monday to Saturday, from 12 noon until 5:30pm on Sundays. The Gardens and Grounds close at 5:15 daily. The times of the tours are from 11am until 4pm from Monday to Saturday and from 1pm until 4pm on

Sundays. The Center is closed on the holidays.

Admission is $16.50 for adults, $13 for seniors (+65),

students (13 to 18), and college students with valid IDs.

For youth (4-12) the admission price is $11.

🌍 Children's Museum of Atlanta

275 Centennial Olympic Park Drive, Atlanta, GA 30303

+1 404-659-5437

http://www.childrensmuseumatlanta.org/

The mission and goal of this museum is to inform kids of

the world around them. It houses hand-on exhibits where

children can explore and discover. There are also a

number of activities which will keep you and your young

ones busy and engaged for hours. Some exhibits at the

Museum include: Body Carnival: the science and fun of

being you, Fundamentally Food, Crawl Space, and Tools

for Solutions where kids can figure out different means

and methods to solve a problem.

Tickets for the museum are priced at $12.75 for everyone.

Toddlers aged 11 months and younger are free to enter

but still require a ticket. Working hours are from 10am to

4pm from Monday to Friday, and from 10am to 5pm on

Saturday and Sunday.

🌑 Zoo Atlanta

800 Cherokee Ave SE, Atlanta, GA 30315

+1 404-624-9453

http://www.zooatlanta.org/

This world-renowned zoo began in 1889 when a traveling

circus was forced into bankruptcy which left the owner no choice but to sell the animals. A few weeks later, they were bought by a businessman and donated to the city of Atlanta where they were stationed at Grant Park. That small group of animals, roughly 11 kinds of animals in all, transformed the area and turned it into Atlanta's first animal-visiting site. By 1935, there was a plethora of new arrivals filling up the zoo, including Jimmie Walker which was the zoo's first tiger.

Nowadays, Zoo Atlanta is the proud recipient of many state as well as national rewards and acclaim. It is the home to more than 200 species of animals like tigers and lions from the African plains, pandas from the Asian forests, as well as numerous types of mammals, reptiles and amphibians. Also be sure to check out the Ford

African Rain Forest which houses 24 gorillas. It is one of the largest captive populations found in North America.

The zoo is open 365 days and closes on Thanksgiving and Christmas Day. Operation hours are from 9:30am to 5:30pm from Monday to Friday, and from 9:30am to 6:30pm on Saturday and Sunday. Admission fees are $21.99 for adults, $16.99 for children (3-11), $17.99 for seniors (+65), and the military and college rates are $17.99. Children two years old and younger enter for free.

🌐 Fernbank Museum of Natural History

767 Clifton Rd NE, Atlanta, GA 30307

+1 404-929-6300

http://www.fernbankmuseum.org/

The Fernbank Museum of Natural History has room after room filled with cultural and artistic treasures. There is an exhibition about the world's largest dinosaurs called 'Giants of the Mesozoic' which presents visitors with a chance to explore various cultures from around the world. There is another exhibition called 'A Walk through Time in Georgia' which will take you on a journey from the Appalachians to the Okefenokee Swamp to the coastal barrier islands. The museum is also the home to an IMAX Theatre which features entertaining and educational films.

There is also a 900-gallon saltwater aquarium, a rose garden, and a children's wing entitled NatureQuest which opened in March of 2011 which features a new and ground-breaking way of interacting with the habitats and ecosystems found in Georgia.

There is also a dining room that offers a view of the 65-acre hardwood forest which the Museum grew out of. Even as you're walking through the museum, you're learning about history; the floors are made of 40,000 limestone tiles highlighting fossils that date all the way back to the Jurassic era.

If you're planning on visiting the Museum anytime from January from November, then be sure to check out Friday nights where you can attend Martinis & IMAX for cocktails, salsa dancing and a movie.

The Museum's working hours are from 10am to 5pm from Monday to Saturday, and on Sundays the Museum is open from 12 noon until 5pm. Admission is $15 for adults and $13 for children (3-12).

🌍 Carter Center & Presidential Library

Freedom Parkway, Atlanta, GA 30307

+1-404-420-5100

http://www.cartercenter.org/index.html

James Earl "Jimmy" Carter, Jr. served as the 39th President of the United States of America. He was awarded the 2002 Nobel Peace Prize. He is the only president who has received the Prize after leaving office. The Jimmy Carter Library is located in Atlanta about 15 miles from Hartsfield International Airport. It mainly holds material belonging to President Carter and his wife Rosalynn and materials pertaining to important figures during Carter's presidency or even his close friends.

ATLANTA TRAVEL GUIDE

The Museum of the Jimmy Carter Library houses photographs of significant events and figures plus memorabilia dating to the time of the Carter presidency. It includes interpretative text, oral histories, and interviews from the Carter White House. The Library also features the gifts that were given to Carter during his presidency. Furthermore there is a model of the Oval Office.

The Carter Center is open every day of the year except on Thanksgiving, Christmas, and New Year's Day. Museum hours are from 9am to 4:45pm Monday through Saturday, and on Sunday from 12 noon to 4:45. The library hours are from Monday through Friday, from 8:30am until 4:30pm. Admission is $8 for adults, $6 for seniors, students and military with ID. Visitors who are 16 years old and younger enter for free. There is free parking available.

🌐 CNN Center & Studio Tour

1 CNN Center, 190 Marietta Street,

NW, Atlanta, GA 30348

+1-404-827-2300

http://edition.cnn.com/tour/

The CNN Center is open to everyone, young and old. If you'd like to walk into the cable news center without going on a tour you won't be charged because entry to the building is free. There are a large number of restaurants where you can stop for lunch. There are also otherservices located in the public area like specialty retail.

ATLANTA TRAVEL GUIDE

If you'd like a tour, however, there are two to choose from.
There is the CNN VIP Tour which runs daily except on
Sundays. This extraordinary tour includes a visit to the
CNN newsroom where you can have your picture taken
as you're sitting at the CNN news desk and studios.

You will also learn about how news and different
programs are recorded at the center and then
broadcasted via satellite all over the world. The second
tour is the Morning Express tour which runs on Thursdays
only. You will get a chance to see the Headline News
Control Room where the magic happens and witness a
live broadcast in action. You will also get a CNN travel
mug and souvenir pictures. Children under the age of 12
are not allowed on this tour.

The hours of the CNN tours are from Monday to Sunday starting at 9am until 5pm. Tickets are sold for $15 for adults, $14 for seniors (+65) and students (13-18 or with college ID), $12 for children (4-12). There are also prices for group trips to the Center. If it's an adult group with twenty or more people then tickets are priced at $13 for each person and if it's a group of children made up of twenty or more children aged 4-12, then tickets are priced at $11 for each child.

Centennial Olympic Park

265 Park Ave West N.W.,

Atlanta, Georgia 30313-1591

+1-404.223.4412

http://www.centennialpark.com/

The Olympic Park was the centerpiece of the 1996 Summer Olympic Games and today is where you can find year-round entertainment and events.

Three million visitors visit the park each year. Anytime of the year you will find the park brimming with excitement and anticipation at the myriad of concerts, fund-raisers, festivals and family activities. The Park sponsors free events for the community like the celebrations which are held on the Fourth of July as well as the weekly alfresco shows like the Wednesday Wind Down concert series and Fourth Saturday Family Fun Days. The Park is the proud owner of the world's largest Olympic Ring fountain.

ATLANTA TRAVEL GUIDE

The Park lies across 21 acres and is within walking distance of the Children's Museum of Atlanta, the World of Coca-Cola, the Georgia Aquarium, and much more. There is free Wi-Fi in and around the Park's Visitor Center. The park opens from 7am until 11pm daily including holidays. General admission is free.

Budget Tips

🌐 Accommodation

Super 8 Atlanta Airport Hotel

2010 Sullivan Road, College Park, GA 30337

+1 770.991.8985

www.atlantaairportsuper8.com

ATLANTA TRAVEL GUIDE

This hotel is one mile away from Hartsfield International Airport and it offers a complimentary shuttle service.

It is only 10 minutes away from downtown Atlanta and all the exciting attractions that await you there such as the CNN studio tour, The World of Coca-Cola, Georgia Aquarium, or Zoo Atlanta. Stone Mountain is also a few minutes away from Super 8 Atlanta Airport Hotel as are the campuses of Georgia State University and Georgia Tech. if you feel like dining there are a handful of restaurants just a brief stroll away.

There are numerous amenities provided by the hotel such as complimentary continental breakfast, satellite TV, a fitness center, a laundry service, an in-room coffee maker and hair dryer. There is also Wi-Fi, a meeting room, and a business center. The average price for a double room per night is $59.

Marriott Atlanta Airport

4711 Best Road, Atlanta, GA 30337

+1-404-766-7900

http://www.marriott.com/hotels/travel/atlap-atlanta-airport-marriott/

Located in a charming and scenic venue on 14 acres, this hotel provides the comfort and convenience that guests are looking for. The rooms are spacious and clean, and all come with a 32 inch flat screen panel LCD TV, deluxe bedding and soundproof windows to ensure that guests get a quiet, relaxing stay. There is also an in-room coffee-maker.

There is a steakhouse on the grounds as well as a sushi bar. The hotel is only minutes from many attractions such as Zoo Atlanta, Georgia Aquarium, Stone Mountain, Martin Luther King, Jr. Center and many more. Prices range from $79 per night.

Crown Plaza Ravinia

4355 Ashford Dunwoody Road, Atlanta, GA 30346

+1 770-395-7700

http://www.cpravinia.com/

Its fantastic location is only one of so many wonderful qualities of this hotel. It is surrounded by a wooded area with the aim of giving its visitors a break from the busy hustle and bustle of the city.

ATLANTA TRAVEL GUIDE

Yet at the same time, it is near Buckhead with its lively art galleries, stores and nightlife. Many attractions are easy to get to via MARTA which is a mere two blocks away from the hotel. The hotel also offers business guests a commute to downtown Atlanta with all its thriving business companies including IBM, T-Mobile, Phillips and UPS.

The hotel offers first-class quality amenities including an indoor pool, a sauna, a fitness center, Wi-Fi, a restaurant, a bar, newspapers, laundry and dry cleaning services, and many more.

Prices range from $80 per night.

Highland Inn

644 N. Highland Avenue, N.E., Atlanta, GA 30306

+1 404-874-5756

http://www.thehighlandinn.com/

When you stay at The Highland Inn, you're guaranteed high quality accommodations. The hotel was first in 1927 and has 80 rooms. It's located in a pedestrian-friendly area within walking distance of numerous restaurants, galleries, bars, and shops. There is a gift shop located on the main level of the hotel. And the pride of the Highland Inn is definitely The Highland Inn Ballroom Lounge which is reserved for events and meetings. It is located beneath the hotel and comes with its private, open-air courtyard, a disco ball, dance floor, and many more amenities

The hotel provides complimentary breakfast, cable TV, Wi-Fi, an iron, ironing board and hair dryer, and so much more. Prices range from $86 for a single room to $110 for

a suite per night.

Days Inn, Atlanta Marietta Galleria

4502 Circle 75 Parkway

Atlanta, GA 30339

1-770-541-9399

http://www.daysinn.com/hotels/georgia/atlanta/days-inn-atlanta-marietta-galleria/hotel-overview

The wonderful thing about this hotel is how it is near to everything else. It's minutes away from Cumberland Mall, and Buckhead where all the great restaurants, shopping centers, and buzzing nightlife are. The rooms are clean and comfortable. The hotel offers complimentary breakfast and USA Today for guests. There is an indoor swimming pool and a fitness center. There is ironing and a dry cleaning service. The hotel also has Wi-Fi and internet service. Prices start at $39 per night.

🌐 Restaurants, Cafés & Bars

Sun Dial Restaurant, Bar & View

Westin Peachtree Plaza

210 Peachtree Street NE, Atlanta, GA 30303

+1- 404- 589-7506

www.sundialrestaurant.com/

This great venue has three aspects. There is a restaurant, a bar, and a viewing area. The Sun Dial can accommodate parties and special events for up to 650 people. There is a children's menu with prices at $8.95 for lunch and $11.95 for dinner. There are vegetarian options on the menus as well as accommodations for special diets.

There have been many awards presented to the Sun Dial Restaurant, Bar & View, like the www.OpenTable.com Diner's Choice Winner in November 2011.

The Sun Dial Restaurant, Bar & View is completely a no-smoking area. The dress code for the Sun Dial is business casual attire in the evening. The Restaurant offers fine cuisine and a great array of dishes served in an elegant setting. The Restaurant hours are from 11:30am to 2:30pm from Monday through Saturday for lunch; the dinner hours are from 6pm to 10pm from Sunday to Thursday, 6pm to 11pm on Friday, and 5:30pm to 11pm on Saturday.

The Bar offers cocktails and a wine list which won an Award of Excellence in 2004 for 'Outstanding Restaurant Wine List' by Wine Spectator.

Every Wednesday and Thursday evenings from 7 to 11 pm, you can enjoy the soft, smooth jazz sounds of the Mose Davis Trio performing at The Sun Dial Restaurant, Bar & View. The Sun Dial also offers cakes from which you can order at $45 and will serve up to 15 people. There are also Sun Dial souvenir glasses available for $14.95 with any drink order.

Being whisked away to 723 ft is just the start of a thrilling ride to get to The View. Once you get to the uppermost level of The Westin Peachtree Plaza, you will be standing atop the tallest building in the Western Hemisphere. The

View offers four complimentary telescopes to gaze out into Atlanta's landmarks, parks, and natural features. You get a 360-degree panoramic, uninhibited view of Atlanta and its skyline. The View hours are from 10am until closing time every day and the price is $6 for adults, $3 for children (6-12).

Alma Cocina

191 Peachtree Street NE, Atlanta, GA 30303

+1-404-968-9662

www.alma-atlanta.com

This restaurant specializes in Mexican cuisine. The food is delightfully fresh and the ingredients all merge into an exploration filled with provincial inspiration.

The dishes are pulsating with flavor and zest. The restaurant specializes in Latin-influenced cocktails and unique tequila. Prices range from $6 - $28.

Anis Café & Bistro

2974 Grandview Ave., Atlanta, GA 30305

+1-404-23309889

www.anisbistro.com

This charming and romantic café and bistro provides cuisines from the French Mediterranean area. The dishes that are served are made with fresh ingredients that exude a delicious aroma and a luscious taste. Anis Café and Bistro has a dining room, an outside patio area, and a bar, it is one of the most romantic dining spots in Atlanta.

Prices for the dinner menu range from $7 to $32.

Alfredo's Italian Restaurant

1989 Cheshire Bridge Rd., Atlanta, GA 30324

+1- 404-876-1380

www.alfredosatlanta.com

Open since 1874, this one-of-a-kind restaurant serves food that entices your taste buds. If you're a fan of Italy and its authentic cuisine, this is the place to go.

You will find all of your favorite Italian dishes, and maybe even discover a few more favorites during your dining experience. There is everything from veal, pastas, fresh seafood in addition to desserts that are homemade, cocktails, and wines. Alfredo's will take you on a romantic trip to Italy and all its sultry, romantic cities without having to leave the comfort of your seat.

Aja

3500 Lenox Rd., Atlanta, GA 30326

+1- 404-231-0001

http://h2sr.com/aja/

This restaurant specializes in Asian cuisine and has earned itself the reputation of being one of Atlanta's most modern and most original Asian restaurant concepts. It first opened in 2008 and is famous for its vibrant bar scene, elaborate décor, and exquisite cuisine. The restaurant consists of a dining room comprised of two stories with a 10ft brass Buddha, a patio area and a

Private dining room which can seat up to 50 guests.

Prices range from 47-$26.

Aqua Blue Restaurant & Bar

1564 Holcomb Bridge Rd., Roswell, GA 30076

www.aquablueatl.com

This restaurant and bar combo offers cuisine from all around the world. You can have your pick of steaks, fresh seafood, chops, and so much more.

The restaurant offers and ambience of exquisite interior with its curtain walls, floors made of bamboo and a high ceiling. The prices are great too and range from $3-$32. The restaurant is open every day from 4pm until 10pm.

🌐 Shopping

Junkman's Daughter

464 Moreland Ave NE, Atlanta, GA 30307

+1- 404-577-3188

http://www.thejunkmansdaughter.com/

If you want to go to a novelty shop that sells everything you can imagine – and some that never even crossed your mind – then head to the Junkman's Daughter. This charming little store opened in 1982 when Pam Majors filled a 1,000 square foot store with 'stuff' she and her parents had accumulated over the years.

This store recently was named one of the 25 Best Independent stores in America. It is celebrating 30 years of being in business and has expanded from being 1,000 square feet to over 10,000 square feet. It is packed full with all sorts of collectibles, knick-knacks, toys, books, and so much more!

Fab'rik

1114 W. Peachtree Street

Atlanta, GA 30309

+1- 404-881-8223

www.fabrikstyle.com

This wonderfully charming boutique offers a fresh and novel shopping experience. Fab'rik is dedicated to offering a unique shopping experience for every person who walks through its doors. All the merchandise is priced under $100 except for the vast denim collection. It promises to deliver the high styled clothes you've seen on the runway or in a fashion magazine without paying the huge sum that being fashionable usually entails. It works, however, on a first-come, first-serve basis, so you have to be quick and on the look-out for that perfect outfit.

North Georgia Premium Outlets

800 Highway 400 South

Dawsonville, GA 30534

+1-706-216-3609

http://www.premiumoutlets.com/outlets/outlet.asp?id=16

This outlet center houses over 140 stores and boutiques. It is considered to be Georgia's only upscale outlet center. Theses shops offer daily savings on their merchandise ranging from 25% off to 65% off.

Walking through this outlet center, you will find brand names as Baby Gap Outlet, Banana Republic Factory Store, Crate and Barrel, Nine West. And that's just to name a few. The outlet center opens starts its shopping hours on regular days from 10am to 9pm from Monday through Saturday and on Sunday from 11am to 7pm.

Cumberland Mall

1000 Cumberland Mall, Atlanta, GA

+1-770-435-2206

Mon. - Sat. 9 a.m. - 9 p.m.; Sun. 12 - 6 p.m.

http://www.cumberlandmall.com/

One of the busiest malls of Atlanta, Cumberland Mall offers you everything from stores carrying accessories to children's apparel to sports and fitness. There is also a car rental store and a mail office. If you're shopping for something particular or if you just want to take a stroll through the aisles, then Cumberland Mall won't let you down.

This mall has a lot of cafes, coffee houses and restaurants. Whether you're in the mood for cheesecake at The Cheesecake Factory or tacos from Taco Bell, you're sure to find it at Cumberland Mall's outdoor plaza, or at any one of the mall's two levels. There are always sales being offered daily at the mall's countless stores.

And to add to the fun, the mall is next to Centennial Olympic Park, the Georgia Aquarium, Zoo Atlanta, and a lot more!

Lenox Square

3393 Peachtree Road NE, Atlanta, GA 30326

+1-404-233-6767

http://www.simon.com/mall/lenox-square

This shopping mall is overflowing with famous and fashionable brand names, restaurants to satiate every palate as well as great deals, news and events. If you want to grab a quick snack or you're in the mood for a scrumptious cupcake, then you'll find what you're looking for. There's even a Japanese restaurant as well as a restaurant which offers 'authentic Russian cuisine'.

Promising to offer a 'legendary shopping' experience, Lenox Square has been noted as the Southeast's chief shopping location for more than forty years. Walking through the mall's four levels you will notice names like

Bloomingdales, Nieman Marcus, Burberry and a whole lot

more.

Know Before You Go

🌐 Entry Requirements

The Visa Waiver Programme (VWP) allows nationals of selected countries to enter the United States for tourism or certain types of business without requiring a visa. This applies to citizens of the UK, Australia, New Zealand, Canada, Chile, Denmark, Belgium, Austria, Latvia, Estonia, Finland, Italy, Hungary, Iceland, France, Germany, Japan, Spain, Portugal, Norway, Sweden, Slovenia, Slovakia, Switzerland, Brunei, Taiwan, South Korea, Luxemburg, Singapore, Liechtenstein, Monaco, Malta, San Marino, Lithuania, Greece, the Netherlands and the Czech Republic. To qualify, you will also need to have a passport with integrated chip, also known as an e-Passport. The e-Passport symbol has to be clearly displayed on the cover of the passport. This secure method of identification will protect and verify the holder in case of identity theft and other breaches of privacy. There are exceptions. Visitors with a criminal record, serious communicable illness or those who were deported or refused entry on a past occasion will not qualify for the Visa Waiver Program and will need to apply for a visa. Holders of a UK passport who have dual citizenship of Iraq, Iran, Sudan, Syria, Somalia, Libya or Yemen (or those who have travelled to the above countries after 2011) will also need to apply for a visa. A requirement of the Visa Waiver Programme is online registration with the Electronic System for Travel Authorisation (ESTA) at least 72 hours before your travels. When entering the United States, you will be able to skip the custom declaration and proceed directly to an Automated Passport Control (APC) kiosk.

If travelling from a non-qualifying country, you will need a visitor's visa, also known as a non-immigrant visa when entering the United States for visiting friends or family, tourism or medical procedures. It is recommended that you schedule your visa interview at least 60 days before your date of travel. You will need to submit a passport that will be valid for at least 6 months after your intended travel, a birth certificate, a police certificate and color photographs that comply with US visa requirements. Proof of financial support for your stay in the United States is also required.

Health Insurance

Medical procedures are very expensive in the United States and there is no free or subsidized healthcare service. The best strategy would be to organize temporary health insurance for the duration of your stay. You will not need any special vaccinations if visiting the United States as tourists. For an immigration visa, the required immunizations are against hepatitis A and B, measles, mumps, rubella, influenza, polio, tetanus, varicella, meningococcal, pneumococcal, rotavirus, pertussis and influenza type B.

There are several companies that offer short-term health insurance packages for visitors to the United States. Coverage with Inbound USA can be purchased online through their website and offer health insurance for periods from 5 to 364 days. Visitor Secure will provide coverage for accidents and new health complications from 5 days to 2 years, but the cost and care of pre-existing medical conditions and dental care is excluded. Inbound Guest offers similar terms for periods of between 5 and 180 days and will email you a virtual membership card as soon as the contract is finalized. Physical cards will be available within one business day of arrival to the United States.

Traveling with Pets

The United States accepts EU pet passports as valid documentation for pets in transit, provided that your pet is up to date on vaccinations. In most instances, the airline you use will require a health certificate. While microchipping is not required, it may be helpful in case your pet gets lost. If visiting from a non-English speaking country, be sure to have an English translation of your vet's certificate available for the US authorities to examine. To be cleared for travel, your pet must have a vet's certificate issued no less than 10 days before your date of travel. Pets need to be vaccinated against rabies at least 30 days prior to entry to the United States. If the animal was recently microchipped, the microchipping procedure should have taken place prior to vaccination. In the case of dogs, it is also important that your pet must test negative for screwworm no later than 5 days before your intended arrival in the United States.

In the case of exotic pets such as parrots, turtles and other reptiles, you will need check on the CITES (Convention on International Trade in Endangered Species of Wild Fauna and Flora) status of the breed, to ensure that you will in fact be allowed to enter the United States with your pet. There are restrictions on bringing birds from certain countries and a quarantine period of 30 days also applies for birds, such as parrots. It is recommended that birds should enter the United States at New York, Los Angeles or Miami, where quarantine facilities are available. The owner of the bird will carry the expense of the quarantine and advance reservations need to be made for this, to prevent the bird being refused entry altogether. Additionally, you will need to submit documentation in the form of a USDA import permit as well as a health certificate issued by your veterinarian less than 30 days prior to the date of entry.

Airports

Your trip will probably be via one of the country's major gateway airports. **Hartsfield–Jackson Atlanta International Airport** (ATL), which is located less than 12km from the central business area of Atlanta in Georgia is the busiest airport in the United States and the world. It processes about 100 million passengers annually. Internationally, it offers connections to Paris, London, Frankfurt Amsterdam, Dubai, Tokyo, Mexico City and Johannesburg. Domestically, its busiest routes are to Florida, New York, Los Angeles, Dallas and Chicago. Delta Airlines maintains a huge presence at the airport, with the largest hub to be found anywhere in the world and a schedule of almost a thousand daily flights. Via a railway station, the airport provides easy access to the city.

Los Angeles International Airport (LAX) is the second busiest airport in the United States and the largest airport in the state of California. Located in the southwestern part of Los Angeles about 24km from the city center, it is easily accessibly by road and rail. Its nine passenger terminals are connected through a shuttle service. Los Angeles International Airport is a significant origin-and-destination airport for travellers to and from the United States. The second busiest airport in California is **San Francisco International Airport** (SFO) and, like Los Angeles it is an important gateway for trans-Pacific connections. It serves as an important maintenance hub for United and is home to an aviation museum. Anyone who is serious about green policies and environmentally friendly alternatives will love San Francisco's airport. There is a special bicycle route to the airport, designated bicycle parking zones and even a service that offers special freight units for travelling with your bicycle. Bicycles are also allowed on its Airtrain service. The third airport of note in California is **San Diego International Airport** (SAN).

Chicago O'Hare International Airport (ORD) is located about 27km northwest of Chicago's central business district, also known as the Chicago Loop. As a gateway to Chicago and the Great Lakes region, it is the US airport that sees the highest frequency of arrivals and departures. Terminal 5 is used for all international arrivals and most international departures, with the exception of Air Canada and some airline carriers under the Star

Alliance or Oneworld brand. The Airport Transit System provides easy access for passengers between terminals and to the remote sections of the parking area.

Located roughly halfway between the cities of Dallas and Fort Worth, **Dallas-Fort Worth International Airport** (DFW) is the primary international airport serving the state of Texas. Both in terms of passenger numbers and air traffic statistics, it ranks among the ten busiest airports in the world. It is also home to the second largest hub in the world, that of American Airlines, which is headquartered in Texas. Through 8 Interstate highways and 3 major rail services, it provides access to the city centers of both Dallas and Fort Worth, as well as the rest of Texas. An automated people mover, known as the Skylink makes it effortless for passenger to transverse between different sections of the airport and the parking areas. Terminal D is its international terminal. The second busiest airport in Texas is the **George Bush Intercontinental Airport** (IAH) in Houston, which offers connections to destinations across the United States, as well as Mexico, Canada, the Americas and selected cities in Europe and Asia.

John F. Kennedy International Airport (JFK) is located in the neighborhood of Queens. In terms of international passengers, it is one of the busiest airports in the United States, with connections to 6 continents and with the air traffic of 70 different airlines. Its busiest routes are to London, Paris, Los Angeles and San Francisco. It serves as a gateway hub for both Delta and American Airlines. Terminal 8, its newest terminal, is larger than Central Park. It has the capacity of processing around 1600 passengers per hour. An elevated railway service, the Airtrain provides access to all 8 of its terminals and also connects to the Long Island railroad as well as the New York City Subway in Queens. Within the airport, the service is free. Three other major airports also service the New York City area. **Newark Liberty International Airport** (EWR) is New York's second busiest airport and home of the world's third largest hub, that of United Airlines. Newark is located about 24km from Mid Manhattan, between Newark and Elizabeth. Its airtrain offers an easy way of commuting around the airport and connects via the Newark Liberty International Airport Station to the North Jersey Coast line and Northeast Corridor line. Other airports in New York are **La Guardia Airport** (LGA), located on the Flushing Bay Waterfront in Queens and **Teterboro Airport** (TEB), which is mainly used by private charter companies.

Washington D.C. is served by two airports, **Baltimore-Washington International Airport** (BWI) and **Washington Dulles International Airport** (IAD). Other important airports on the eastern side of the United States include **Logan International Airport** (BOS) in Boston, **Philadelphia International Airport** (PHL) and **Charlotte Douglas International Airport** (CLT) in North Carolina. The three busiest airports in the state of Florida are **Miami International Airport** (MIA), **Fort Lauderdale-Hollywood International Airport** (FLL) and **Tampa International Airport** (TPA). In the western part of the United States, **McCarran International Airport** (LAS) in Las Vegas and **Phoenix Sky Harbor International** (PHX) in Arizona offer important connections. **Denver International Airport** (DEN) in Colorado is the primary entry point to Rocky Mountains, while **Seattle-Tacoma International Airport** (SEA) in Washington State and **Portland International Airport** (PDX) in Oregon provide access to the Pacific Northwest. **Honolulu International Airport** (HNL) is the primary point of entry to Hawaii.

Airlines

The largest air carriers in the United States are United Airlines, American Airlines and Delta Airlines. Each of these could lay claim to the title of largest airline using different criteria. In terms of passenger numbers, Delta Airlines is the largest airline carrier. It was founded from humble beginnings as a crop dusting outfit in the 1920s, but grew to an enormous operation through mergers with Northeast Airlines in the 1970s, Western Airlines in the 1980s and North-western Airlines in 2010. Delta also absorbed a portion of Pan Am's assets and business, following its bankruptcy in the early 1990s. Delta Airlines operates Delta Connections, a regional service covering North American destinations in Canada, Mexico and the United States. In terms of destinations, United Airlines is the largest airline in the United States and the world. Its origins lie in an early airline created by Boeing in the 1920s, but the company grew from a series of acquisitions and mergers - most recently with Continental Airlines - to its current status as a leading airline. Regional services are operated under the brand United Express, in partnership with a range of feeder carriers including CapeAir, CommutAir, ExpressJet, GoJet Airlines, Mesa Airlines, Republic Airlines, Shuttle America, SkyWest Airlines and Trans State Airlines. American Airlines commands the largest fleet in the United States. It originated from the merger of over 80 tiny regional airlines in the 1930s and has subsequently merged with Trans Caribbean Airways, Air California, Reno Air, Trans World Airlines and, most recently, US Airways. Through the Oneworld Airline Alliance, American Airlines is partnered with British Airways, Finnair, Iberia and Japan Airlines. Regional connections are operated under the American Eagle brand name and include the services of Envoy

Air, Piedmont Airlines, Air Wisconsin, SkyWest Airlines, Republic Airlines and PSA Airlines. American Airlines operates the American Airlines Shuttle, a service that connects the cities of New York, Boston and Washington DC with hourly flights on weekdays.

Based in Dallas, Texas, Southwest Airlines is the world's largest budget airline. It carries the highest number of domestic passengers in the United States and operates over 200 daily flights on its 3 busiest routes, namely Chicago, Washington and Las Vegas. JetBlue Airways is a budget airline based in Long Island that operates mainly in the Americas and the Caribbean. It covers 97 destinations in the United States, Mexico, Costa Rica, Puerto Rico, Grenada, Peru, Colombia, Bermuda, Jamaica, the Bahamas, Barbados, the Dominican Republic and Trinidad and Tobago. Spirit Airlines is an ultra low cost carrier which offers flights to destinations in the United States, Latin America, Mexico and the Caribbean. It is based in Miramar, Florida.

Alaska Airlines was founded in the 1930s to offer connections in the Pacific Northwest, but began to expand from the 1990s to include destinations east of the Rocky Mountains as well as connections to the extreme eastern part of Russia. Alaska Airlines recently acquired the brand, Virgin America which represents the Virgin brand in the United States. Silver Airways is a regional service which offers connections to various destinations in Florida, Pennsylvania, Virginia and West Virginia and provides a service to several islands within the Bahamas. Frontier Airlines is a relatively new budget airline that is mainly focussed on connections around the Rocky Mountain states. Hawaiian Airlines is based in Honolulu and offers connections to the American mainland as well as to Asia. Island Air also serves Hawaii and enjoys a partnership with United Airlines. Mokulele Airlines is a small airline based in Kona Island. It provides access to some of the smaller airports in the Hawaiian Islands. Sun Country Airlines is based in Minneapolis and covers destinations in the United States, Mexico, Costa Rica, Puerto Rica, Jamaica, St Maarten and the US Virgin Islands. Great Lakes Airline is a major participant in the Essential Air Service, a government programme set up to ensure that small and remote communities can be reached by air, following the deregulation of certified airlines. These regional connections include destinations in Arizona, Colorado, Kansas, Minnesota, Nebraska, New Mexico, South Dakota and Wyoming. In the past, Great Lakes Airline had covered a wide range of destinations as a partner under the United Express banner.

ATLANTA TRAVEL GUIDE

🌐 **Hubs**

Hartsfield Jackson Atlanta International Airport serves as the largest hub and headquarters of Delta Airlines. John F. Kennedy International Airport serves as a major hub for Delta's traffic to and from the European continent. Los Angeles International Airport serves as a hub for Delta Airline's connections to Mexico, Hawaii and Japan, but also serves the Florida-California route. Detroit Metropolitan Wayne County Airport is Delta's second largest hubs and serves as a gateway for connections to Asia.

Washington Dulles International Airport serves as a hub for United Airlines as well as Silver Airways. United Airlines also use Denver International Airport, George Bush Intercontinental Airport in Houston, Los Angeles International Airport, San Francisco International Airport, Newark Liberty International Airport and O'Hare International Airport in Chicago as hubs.

Dallas/Fort Worth International Airport serves as the primary hub for American Airlines. Its second largest hub in the south-eastern part of the US is Charlotte Douglas International Airport in North Carolina and its largest hub in the north is O'Hare International Airport in Chicago. Other hubs for American Airlines are Phoenix Sky Harbor International Airport - its largest hub in the west - Miami International Airport, Ronald Reagan Washington National Airport, Los Angeles International Airport, John F Kennedy International Airport in New York, which serves as a key hub for European air traffic and La Guardia Airport also in New York.

Seattle-Tacoma International Airport serves as a primary hub for Alaska Airlines. Other hubs for Alaska include Portland International Airport, Los Angeles International Airport and Ted Stevens - Anchorage International Airport. Virgin America operates a primary hub at San Francisco International Airport, but also has a second hub at Los Angeles International Airport as well as a significant presence at Dallas Love Field. Denver International Airport is the primary hub for Frontier Airlines, which also has hubs at Chicago O'Hare International Airport and Orlando International Airport. Frontier also maintains a strong presence at Hartsfield-Jackson Atlanta International Airport, Cincinnati/North Kentucky International Airport, Cleveland Hopkins International Airport, McCarran International Airport in Las Vegas and Philadelphia International Airport. Honolulu International Airport and Kahului Airport serve as hubs for Hawaiian Airlines. Mokulele Airlines uses Kona International Airport and Kahului Airport as hubs. Minneapolis–Saint Paul International Airport serves as a hub for Delta Airlines, Great Lakes Airlines and Sun Country

Airlines. Silver Airways uses Fort Lauderdale-Hollywood International Airport as a primary hub and also has hubs at Tampa International Airport, Orlando International Airport and Washington Dulles International Airport.

☻ Seaports

The Port of Miami is often described as the cruise capital of the world, but it also serves as a cargo gateway to the United States. There are 8 passenger terminals and the Port Miami Tunnel, an undersea tunnel connects the port to the Interstate 95 via the Dolphin Expressway. Miami is an important base for several of the world's most prominent cruise lines, including Norwegian Cruise Lines, Celebrity Cruises, Royal Caribbean International and Carnival Cruises. In total, over 40 cruise ships representing 18 different cruise brands are berthed at Miami. Well over 4 million passengers are processed here annually. There are two other important ports in the state of Florida. Port Everglades is the third busiest cruise terminal in Florida, as well as its busiest cargo terminal. It is home to *Allure of the Seas* and *Oasis of the Seas*, two of the world's largest cruise ships. Oceanfront condominium dwellers often bid ships farewell with a friendly cacophony of horns and bells. The third important cruise port in Florida is Port Canaveral, which has 5 cruise terminals.

With its location on the Mississippi river, New Orleans is an important cargo port, but it also has a modern cruise terminal with over 50 check-in counters. The Port of Seattle is operated by the same organization that runs the city's airport. It has two busy cruise terminals. The Port of Los Angeles has a state of the art World Cruise Center, with three berths for passenger liners. As the oldest port on the Gulf of Mexico, the Port of Galveston dates back to the days when Texas was still part of Mexico. Galveston serves both as a cargo port and cruise terminal.

Money Matters

Currency

The currency of the United States is US dollar (USD). Notes are issued in denominations of $1, $2, $5, $10, $20, $50 and $100. Coins are issued in denominations of $1 (known as a silver dollar, 50c (known as a half dollar), 25c (quarter), 10c (dime), 5c (nickel) and 1c (penny).

⊕ Banking/ATMs

ATM machines are widely distributed across the United States and are compatible with major networks such as Cirrus and Plus for international bank transactions. Most debit cards will display a Visa or MasterCard affiliation, which means that you may be able to use them as a credit card as well. A transaction fee will be charged for withdrawals, but customers of certain bank groups such as Deutsche Bank and Barclays, can be charged smaller transaction fees or none at all, when using the ATM machines of Bank of America. While banking hours will vary, depending on the location and banking group, you can generally expect most banks to be open between 8.30am and 5pm. You will be asked for ID in the form of a passport, when using your debit card for over-the-counter transactions.

While you cannot open a bank account in the United States without a social security number, you may want to consider obtaining a pre-paid debit card, where a fixed amount can be pre-loaded. This service is available from various credit card companies in the United States. The American Express card is called Serve and can be used with a mobile app. You can load more cash at outlets of Walmart, CVS Pharmacy, Dollar General, Family Dollar, Rite Aid and participating 7/Eleven stores.

Credit Cards

Credit cards are widely used in the United States and the the major cards - MasterCard, Visa, American Express and Diners Club – are commonly accepted. A credit card is essential in paying for hotel accommodation or car rental. As a visitor, you may want to check about the fees levied on your card for foreign exchange transactions. While Europe and the UK have already converted to chip-and-pin credit card, the transition is still in progress in the United States. Efforts are being made to make the credit cards of most US stores compliant with chip-and-pin technology. You may find that many stores still employ the older protocols at point-of-sales. Be sure to inform your bank or credit card vendor of your travel plans before leaving home.

Tourist Tax

In the United States, tourist tax varies from city to city, and can be charged not only on accommodation, but also restaurant bills, car rental and other services that cater mainly to tourists. In 22 states, some form of state wide tax is charged for accommodation and 38 states levy a tax on car rental. The city that levies the highest tax bill is Chicago. Apart from a flat fee of $2.75, you can expect to be charged 16 percent per day on hotel accommodation as well as nearly 25% for car rentals. New York charges an 18 percent hotel tax, as does Nashville, while Kansas City, Houston and Indianapolis levy around 17 percent per day hotel tax. Expect to pay 16.5 percent tax per day on your hotel bill in Cleveland and 15.6 percent per day in Seattle, with a 2 percent hike, if staying in the Seattle Tourism Improvement Area. Las Vegas charges 12 percent hotel tax. In Los Angeles, you will be charged a whopping 14 percent on your hotel room, but in Burbank, California, the rate is only 2 percent. Dallas, Texas only charges 2 percent on hotels with more than a hundred rooms. In Portland a city tax of 6 percent is added to a county tax of 5.5 percent. Do inquire about the hotel tax rate in the city where you intend to stay, when booking your accommodation.

◯ Sales Tax

In the United States, the sales tax rate is set at state level, but in most states local counties can set an additional surtax. In some states, groceries and/or prescription drugs will be exempt from tax or charged at a lower rate. There are only five states that charge no state sales tax at all. They are Oregon, Delaware, New Hampshire, Alaska and Montana. Alaska allows a local tax rate not exceeding 7 percent and in Montana, local authorities are enabled to set a surtax rate, should they wish to do so. The state sales tax is generally set at between 4 percent (Alabama, Georgia, Louisiana, and Wyoming) and 7 percent (Indiana, Mississippi, New Jersey, Tennessee, Rhode Island) although there are exceptions outside that spectrum with Colorado at 2.8 percent and California at 7.5 percent. The local surcharge can be anything from 4.7 percent (Hawaii) to around 11 percent (Oklahoma and Louisiana). Can you claim back tax on your US purchases as a tourist? In the United States, sales tax is added retro-actively upon payment, which means that it will not be included in the marked price of the goods you buy. Because it is set at state, rather than federal level, it is usually not refundable.

Two states do offer sales tax refunds to tourists. In Texas you will be able to get tax back from over 6000 participating stores if the tax amount came to more than $12 and the goods were purchased within 30 days of your departure. To qualify, you need to submit the original sales receipts, your passport, flight or transport information and visa details. Refunds are made in cash, cheque or via PayPal. Louisiana was the first state to introduce tax refunds for tourists. To qualify there, you must submit all sales receipts, together with your passport and flight ticket at a Refund Center outlet.

◉ Tipping

Tipping is very common in the United States. In sit-down restaurants, a tip of between 10 and 15 percent of the bill is customary. At many restaurants, the salaries of waiting staff will be well below minimum wage levels. With large groups of diners, the restaurant may charge a mandatory gratuity, which is automatically included in the bill. At the trendiest New York restaurants, a tip of 25 percent may be expected. While you can add a credit card tip, the best way to ensure the gratuity reaches your server is to tip separately in cash. Although tipping is less of an obligation at takeaway restaurants, such as McDonalds, you can leave your change, or otherwise $1, if there is a tip jar on the counter. In the case of pizza delivery, a minimum of $3 is recommended and more is obviously appreciated. Although a delivery charge is often levied, this money usually goes to the pizzeria, rather than the driver. Tip a taxi driver 10 percent of the total fare. At your hotel, tip the porter between $1 and $2 per bag. Tip between 10 and 20 percent at hair salons, spas, beauty salons and barber shops. Tip tour guides between 10 and 20 percent for a short excursion. For a day trip, tip both the guide and the driver $5 to $10 per person, if a gratuity is not included in the cost of the tour. Tip the drivers of charter or sightseeing buses around $1 per person.

Connectivity

Mobile Phones

There are four major service providers for wireless connection in the United States. They are Verizon Wireless, T-Mobile US, AT&T Mobility and Sprint. Not all are compatible with European standards. While most countries in Europe, Asia, the Middle East and East Africa uses the GSM mobile network, only two US service providers, T-Mobile and AT&T Mobility aligns with this. Also bear in mind that GSM carriers in the United States operate using the 850 MHz/1900 MHz frequency bands, whereas the UK, all of Europe, Asia, Australia and Africa use 900/1800MHz. You should check with your phone's tech specifications to find out whether it supports these standards. The other services, Verizon Wireless and Sprint use the CDMA network standard and, while Verizon's LTE frequencies are somewhat compatible with those of T-Mobile and AT&T, Sprint uses a different bandwidth for its LTE coverage.

To use your own phone, you can purchase a T-Mobile 3-in-1 starter kit for $20. If your device is unlocked, GMS-capable and supports either Band II (1900 MHz) or Band IV (1700/2100 MHz), you will be able to access the T-Mobile network. You can also purchase an AT&T sim card through the Go Phone Pay-as-you-go plan for as little as $0.99. Refill cards are available from $25 and are valid for 90 days. If you want to widen your network options, you may want to explore the market for a throwaway or disposable phone. At Walmart, you can buy non-contracted phones for as little as $9.99, as well as pre-paid sim cards and data top-up packages.

Canadians travellers will find the switch to US networks technically effortless, but should watch out for roaming costs. Several American networks do offer special international rates for calls to Canada or Mexico.

Dialing Code

The international dialing code for the United States is +1.

☺ Emergency Numbers

General Emergency: 911 (this number can be used free of charge from any public phone in the United States).
MasterCard: 1-800-307-7309
Visa: 1-800-847-2911

☺ General Information

☺ Public Holidays

1 January: New Year's Day

3rd Monday in January: Martin Luther King Day

3rd Monday in February: President's Day

Last Monday in May: Memorial Day

4 July: Independence Day

1st Monday in September: Labour Day

2nd Monday in October: Columbus Day

11 November: Veteran's Day

4th Thursday in November: Thanksgiving Day

4th Friday in November: Day after Thanksgiving

25 December: Christmas Day (if Christmas Day falls on a Sunday, the Monday thereafter is a public holiday.) In some states, 26 December is a public holiday as well.

There are several festivals that are not public holidays per se, but are culturally observed in the United States. They include:

14 February: Valentine's Day

17 March: St Patrick's Day

March/April (variable): Easter or Passover

Second Sunday in May: Mother's Day

3rd Sunday in June: Father's Day

31 October: Halloween

🌐 Time Zones

The United States has 6 different time zones. **Eastern Standard Time** is observed in the states of Maine, New York, New Hampshire, Delaware, Vermont, Maryland, Rhode Island, Massachusetts, Connecticut, Pennsylvania, Ohio, North Carolina, South Carolina, Georgia, Virginia, West Virginia, Michigan, most of Florida and Indiana as well as the eastern parts of Kentucky and Tennessee. Eastern Standard Time is calculated as Greenwich Meantime/Coordinated Universal Time (UTC) -5. **Central Standard Time** is observed in Iowa, Illinois, Missouri, Arkansas, Louisiana, Oklahoma, Kansas, Mississippi, Alabama, near all of Texas, the western half of Kentucky, the central and western part of Tennessee, sections of the north-western and south-western part of Indiana, most of

North and South Dakota, the eastern and central part of Nebraska and the north-western strip of Florida, also known as the Florida Panhandle. Central Standard Time is calculated as Greenwich Meantime/Coordinated Universal Time (UTC) -6. **Mountain Standard Time** is observed in New Mexico, Colorado, Wyoming, Montana, Utah, Arizona, the southern and central section of Idaho, the western parts of Nebraska, South Dakota and North Dakota, a portion of eastern Oregon and the counties of El Paso and Hudspeth in Texas. Mountain Standard Time is calculated as Greenwich Meantime/Coordinated Universal Time (UTC) -7. **Pacific Standard Time** is used in California, Washington, Nevada, most of Oregon and the northern part of Idaho. Pacific Standard Time is calculated as Greenwich Meantime/Coordinated Universal Time (UTC) -8. **Alaska Standard Time** is used in Alaska and this can be calculated as Greenwich Meantime/Coordinated Universal Time (UTC) -9. Because of its distant location, Hawaii is in a time zone of its own. **Hawaii Standard Time** can be calculated as Greenwich Meantime/Coordinated Universal Time (UTC) - 10.

☺ Daylight Savings Time

Clocks are set forward one hour at 2.00am on the second Sunday of March and set back one hour at 2.00am on the first Sunday of November for Daylight Savings Time. The states of Hawaii and Arizona do not observe Daylight Savings Time. However, the Navajo Indian Reservation, which extends across three states (Arizona, Utah and New Mexico), does observe Daylight Savings Time throughout its lands, including that portion which falls within Arizona.

☺ School Holidays

In the United States, the academic year begins in September, usually in the week just before or after Labour Day and ends in the early or middle part of June. There is a Winter Break that includes Christmas and New Year and a Spring Break in March or April that coincides with Easter. In some states, there is also a Winter Break in February. The summer break occurs in the 10 to 11 weeks between the ending of one academic year and the commencement of the next academic year. Holidays may vary according to state and certain weather conditions such as hurricanes or snowfall may also lead to temporary school closures in affected areas.

ATLANTA TRAVEL GUIDE

☯ Trading Hours

Trading hours in the United States vary. Large superstores like Walmart trade round the clock at many of its outlets, or else between 7am and 10pm. Kmart is often open from 8am to 10pm, 7 days a week. Target generally opens at 8am and may close at 10 or 11pm, depending on the area. Many malls will open at 10am and close at 9pm. Expect restaurants to be open from about 11am to 10pm or 11pm, although the hours of eateries that serve alcohol and bars may be restricted by local legislation. Banking hours also vary, according to branch and area. Branches of the Bank of America will generally open at 9am, and closing time can be anywhere between 4pm and 6pm. Most post office outlets are open from 9am to 5pm on weekdays.

☯ Driving

In the United States, motorists drive on the right hand side of the road. As public transport options are not always adequate, having access to a car is virtually essential, when visiting the United States. To drive, you will need a valid driver's licence from your own country, in addition to an international driving permit. If your driver's licence does not include a photograph, you will be asked to submit your passport for identification as well.

For car rental, you will also need a credit card. Some companies do not rent out vehicles to drivers under the age of 25. Visitors with a UK license may need to obtain a check code for rental companies, should they wish to verify the details and validity of their driver's licence, via the DVLA view-your-licence service. This can also be generated online, but must be done at least 72 hours prior to renting the car. In most cases, though, the photo card type license will be enough. The largest rental companies - Alamo, Avis, Budget, Hertz, Dollar and Thrifty - are well represented in most major cities and usually have offices at international airports. Do check about the extent of cover included in your travel insurance package and credit card agreement. Some credit card companies may include Collision Damage Waiver (CDW), which will cover you against being held accountable for any damage to the rental car, but it is recommended that you also arrange for personal accident insurance, out-of-state insurance and supplementary liability insurance. You can sometimes cut costs on car rentals by reserving a car via the internet before leaving home.

The maximum speed limit in the United States varies according to state, but is usually between 100km per hour (65 m.p.h.) and 120km per hour (75 m.p.h.). For most of the Eastern states, as well as California and Oregon on the west coast the maximum speed driven on interstate highways should be 110km per hour (70 m.p.h.). Urban speed legislation varies, but in business and residential areas, speeds are usually set between 32km (20 miles) and 48km (30 miles) per hour. In Colorado, nighttime speed limits apply in certain areas where migrating wildlife could be endangered and on narrow, winding mountain passes, a limit of 32km (20 miles) per hour sometimes applies. In most American states there is a ban on texting for all drivers and a ban on all cell phone use for novice drivers.

Drinking

It is illegal in all 50 states for persons under the age of 21 to purchase alcohol or to be intoxicated. In certain states, such as Texas, persons between the age of 18 and 21 may be allowed to drink beer or wine, if in the company of a parent or legal guardian. In most states, the trading hours for establishments selling alcohol is limited. There are a few exceptions to this. In Nevada, alcohol may be sold round the clock and with few restrictions other than age. In Louisiana, there are no restrictions on trading in alcohol at state level, although some counties set their own restrictions. By contrast, Arizona has some of the strictest laws in relation to alcohol sales, consumption and driving under the influence. The sale of alcohol is prohibited on Native American reservations, unless the tribal council of that reservation has passed a vote to lift restrictions.

Smoking

There is no smoking ban set at federal level in the United States. At state level, there are 40 states in total that enact some form of state wide restriction on smoking, although the exemptions of individual states may vary. In Arizona, California, Colorado, Connecticut, Delaware, Hawaii, Illinois, Iowa, Kansas, Maine, Maryland, Massachusetts, Michigan, Minnesota, Montana, Nebraska, North Dakota, New Jersey, New Mexico, New York, Ohio, Oregon, Rhode Island, South Dakota, Utah, Vermont, Washington and Wisconsin, smoking is prohibited in all public enclosed areas, including bars and restaurants. The states of Arkansas, Florida, Indiana, Louisiana, Pennsylvania and Tennessee do have a general state wide restriction on smoking in public places, but exempt adult venues where under 21s are not allowed. This includes bars, restaurants, betting shops and gaming parlours (Indiana) and casinos (Louisiana and Pennsylvania). Nevada also has a state wide ban on smoking that exempts casinos, bars, strip clubs and brothels. In Georgia, state wide smoking legislation exempts bars and restaurants that only serve patrons over the age of 18. Idaho has a state wide ban that includes restaurants, but exempts bars serving only alcohol. New Hampshire, North Carolina and Virginia have also introduced some form of state wide smoking restriction. While the states of Alabama, Alaska, Kentucky, Mississippi, Missouri, Oklahoma, South Carolina, Texas, West Virginia and Wyoming have no state legislation, there are more specific restrictions at city and county level. In Arizona, there is an exemption for businesses located on Native American reservation and, in particular, for Native American religious ceremonies that may include smoking rituals. In California, the first state to implement anti-smoking legislation, smoking is also prohibited in parks and on sidewalks.

Electricity

Electricity: 110 volts
Frequency: 60 Hz
Electricity sockets are compatible with American Type A and Type B plugs. The Type A plug features two flat prongs or blades, while the Type B plug has the same plus an additional

'earth' prong. Most newer models of camcorders and cameras are dual voltage, which means that you should be able to charge them without an adapter in the United States, as they have a built in converter for voltage. You may find that appliances from the UK or Europe which were designed to accommodate a higher voltage will not function as effectively in the United States. While a current converter or transformer will be able to adjust the voltage, you may still experience some difficulty with the type of devices that are sensitive to variations in frequency as the United States uses 60 Hz, instead of the 50 Hz which is common in Europe and the UK. Appliances like hairdryers will usually be available in hotels and since electronic goods are fairly cheap in the United States, the easiest strategy may be to simply purchase a replacement. Bear in mind, that you may need an adaptor or transformer to operate it once you return home.

⊙ Food & Drink

Hamburgers, hot dogs and apple pie may be food items that come to mind when considering US culinary stereotypes, but Americans eat a wide variety of foods. They love steaks and ribs when dining out and pancakes or waffles for breakfast. As a society which embraces various immigrant communities,

America excels at adopting and adapting traditional staples and adding its own touch to them. Several "Asian" favorites really originated in the United States. These include the California roll (offered in sushi restaurants) and the fortune cookie (chinese). Popular Hispanic imports include tacos, enchiladas and burritos. Another stereotype of American cuisine is large portion sizes. Hence the existence of American inventions such as the footlong sub, the footlong chilli cheese hot dog and the Krispy Creme burger, which combines a regular hamburger with a donut. Corn dogs are fairground favorites. Most menus are more balanced however. It is common to ask for a doggy bag (to take away remaining food) in a restaurant.

When in the South, enjoy corn bread, grits and southern fried chicken. Try spicy buffalo wings in New York, traditionally prepared baked beans in Boston and deep dish pizza in Chicago. French fries are favorites with kids of all ages, but Americans also love their potatoes as hash browns or the bite sized tater tots. Indulge your sweet tooth with Twinkies, pop tarts, cup cakes and banana splits. Popular sandwiches include the BLT (bacon, lettuce, tomato, the Reuben sandwich, the sloppy joe and the peanut butter and jelly.

Sodas (fizzy drinks) and bottled waters are the top beverages in the United States. The top selling soft drinks are Coca Cola, followed by Pepsi Cola, Diet Coke, Mountain Dew and Dr Pepper. In America's colonial past, tea was initially the hot beverage of choice and it was tea politics that kicked off the American Revolution, but gradually tea has been replaced by coffee in popularity. From the 1970s, Starbucks popularized coffee culture in the United States. Americans still drink gallons of tea and they are particularly fond of a refreshing glass of iced tea. Generally, Americans drink more beer than wine and favorite brands include Bud Light, followed by Coors Light, Budweiser and Miller Light. Popular cocktails are the Martini, the Manhattan, the Margarita, the Bloody Mary, the Long Island Ice tea and Sex on the Beach.

American Sports

Baseball is widely regarded as the national sport of America. The sport originated in the mid 1800s and superficially shares the basic objective of cricket, which is to score runs by hitting a ball pitched by the opposing team, but in baseball, the innings ends as soon as three players have been caught out. A point is scored when a runner has passed three bases and reached the 4th or home base of the baseball diamond. After 9 innings, the team with the highest number of runs is declared the winner. The Baseball World Series is played in the fall (autumn), usually in October, and consists of best-of-seven play-off between the two top teams representing the rival affiliations of the National League and American League.

Although the origins of American football can be found in rugby, the sport is now widely differentiated from its roots and today numerous distinctions exist between the two. In American football, a game is divided into four quarters, with each team fielding 11 players, although unlimited substitution is allowed. Players wear helmets and heavy padding as any player can be tackled, regardless of ball possession. An annual highlight is the Super Bowl, the championship game of the National Football League. The event is televised live to over a 100 million viewers and features a high profile halftime performance by a top music act. Super bowl Sunday traditionally takes place on the first Sunday of February.

The roots of stock car racing can be found in America's prohibition era, when bootleggers needed powerful muscle cars (often with modifications for greater speed) to transport their illicit alcohol stocks. Informal racing evolved to a lively racing scene in Daytona, Florida. An official body, NASCAR, was founded in 1948 to regulate the sport, NASCAR. Today, NASCAR racing has millions of fans. One of its most prestigious events is the Sprint Cup, a championship which comprises of 36 races and kicks off each year with the Daytona 500.

Rodeo originated from the chores and day-to-day activities of Spanish cattle farmers and later, the American ranchers who occupied the former Spanish states such as Texas, California and Arizona. The advent of fencing eliminated the need for cattle drives, but former cowboys found that their skills still offered good entertainment, providing a basis for wild west shows such as those presented by Buffalo Bill. Soon, rodeo events became the highlight of frontier towns throughout the west. During the first half of the 20th centuries, organizations formed to regulate events. Today, rodeo is considered a legitimate national sport with millions of fans. If you want to experience the thrill of this extreme sport, attend one of its top events. The Prescott Frontier Days show in Arizona is billed to be America's oldest rodeo. The Reno Rodeo in Nevada is a 10 day event that takes place in mid-June and includes the option of closer participation as a volunteer. Rodeo Houston, a large 20 day event that takes place towards the end of winter, is coupled to a livestock show. Visit the San Antonio show in Texas during February for the sheer variety of events. The National Western Rodeo in Denver Colorado is an indoor event that attracts up to half a million spectators each year. The National Finals that takes place in Las Vegas during December is the prestigious championship that marks the end of the year's rodeo calendar.

Useful Websites

https://esta.cbp.dhs.gov/esta/ -- The US Electronic System for Travel Authorization

http://www.visittheusa.com/

http://roadtripusa.com/

http://www.roadtripamerica.com/

http://www.road-trip-usa.info/

http://www.autotoursusa.com/

http://www.onlyinyourstate.com/

http://www.theamericanroadtripcompany.co.uk/

Printed in Great Britain
by Amazon